AT THE FEET OF OUR ELDERS

A GUIDED JOURNAL OF 45 INTERVIEW QUESTIONS FOR CONVERSATIONS BETWEEN ADULTS AND THEIR ELDERS

THIS JOURNAL BELONGS TO

_____

Elder 1:

Interview Date(s)

Birthday   Age

Birth City, State, Country

Mother's Name

Father's Name

Sibling's Name(s) & Ages

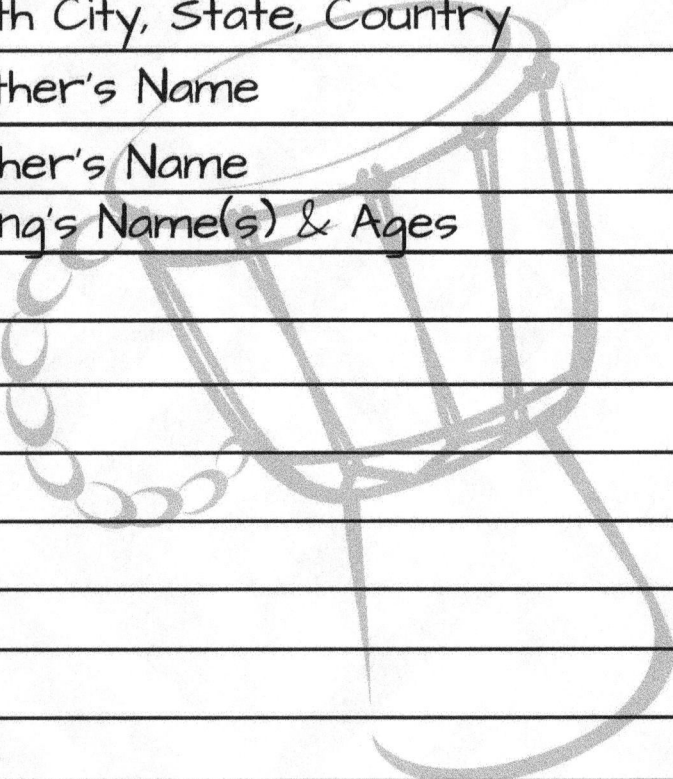

Elder 2:

Interview Date(s)

Birthday   Age

Birth City, State, Country

Mother's Name

Father's Name

Sibling's Name(s) & Ages

When you were a child, what did you dream about doing?

Elder 1:

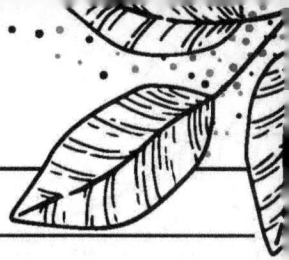

Elder 2:

What would you do differently if you had a second chance?

Elder 1:

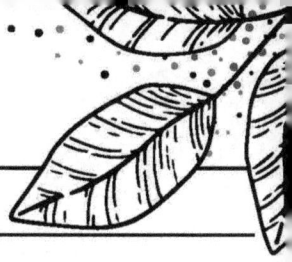

Elder 2:

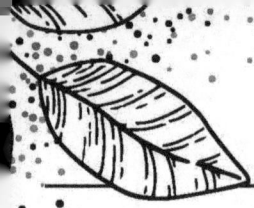

Tell me about a person, outside of our family, who had a positive impact on your life.

Elder 1:

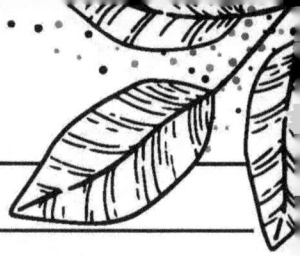

Elder 2:

Tell me about a time you met a
celebrity or tell me about a
celebrity you would like to meet

Elder 1:

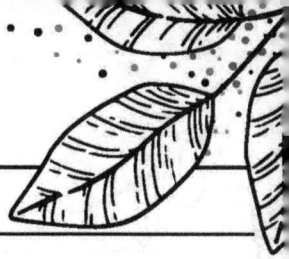

Elder 2:

What did you like to do for fun when you were growing up?

Elder 1:

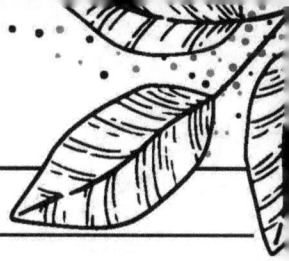

Elder 2:

What major world events have occurred during your lifetime and what was your experience?

Elder 1:

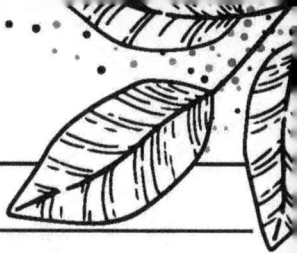

Elder 2:

What places have you traveled to in your lifetime?

Elder 1:

Elder 2:

What is one thing about our family that many people don't know?

Elder 1:

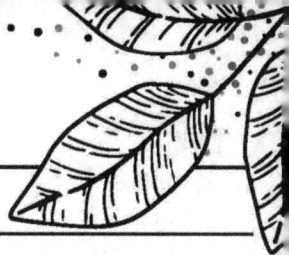

Elder 2:

Tell me what it was like in the town where you grew up.

Elder 1:

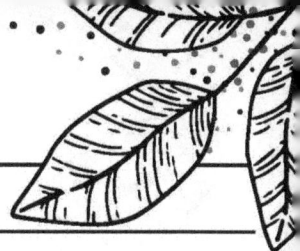

Elder 2:

What's your favorite genre of music?

Elder 1:

Elder 2:

Which decade was your best, so far, and what made it amazing?

Elder 1:

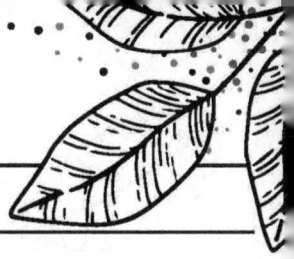

Elder 2:

How has your parenting style been different from your parents?

Elder 1:

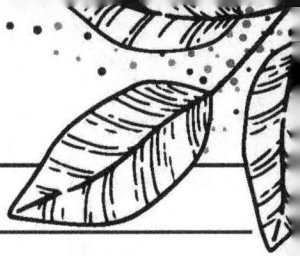

Elder 2:

What do you wish you learned in school that you were never taught?

Elder 1:

Elder 2:

What holidays, if any, were celebrated in your family when growing up?

Elder 1:

Elder 2:

What kind of student were you?

Elder 1:

Elder 2:

What do you think someone would be surprised to know about you?

Elder 1:

Elder 2:

Tell me what you know about our family tree. Let's map it out together!

Elder 1:

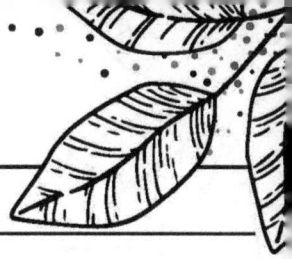

Elder 2:

What are you most proud of so far?

Elder 1:

Elder 2:

What are five things that are on your bucket list?

Elder 1:

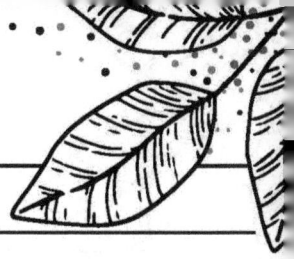

Elder 2:

What gives you a hearty belly laugh every time you hear it, see it or do it?

Elder 1:

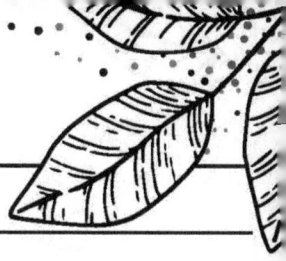

Elder 2:

What advice would you give to people 100 years from now?

Elder 1:

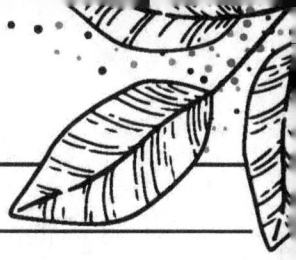

Elder 2:

What advice do you have for the youth of today?

Elder 1:

Elder 2:

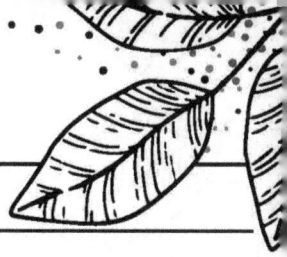

Tell me about a time you overcame a major obstacle.

Elder 1:

Elder 2:

What is one thing about your life that makes you feel proud?

Elder 1:

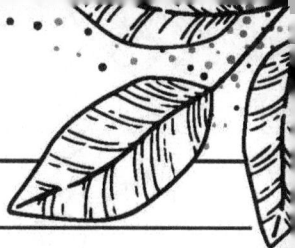

Elder 2:

What are three adjectives you would use to describe yourself?

Elder 1:

Elder 2:

How do you think your friends would describe you?

Elder 1:

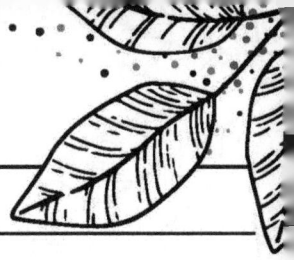

Elder 2:

Tell me something you can do now
that you couldn't do before.

Elder 1:

Elder 2:

Tell me something you could do when you were younger that you wish you could still do now.

Elder 1:

Elder 2:

What was one of the most valuable lessons you learned from your parents?

Elder 1:

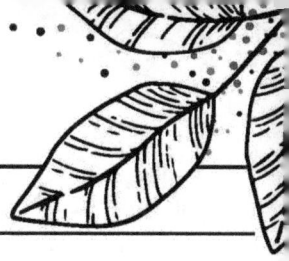

Elder 2:

You're hosting an event with the ten people closest you. Who has a seat at the table?

Elder 1:

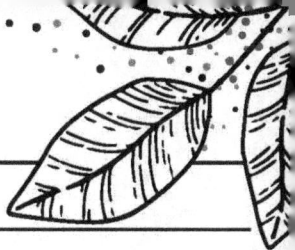

Elder 2:

While growing up, what did you enjoy learning most?

Elder 1:

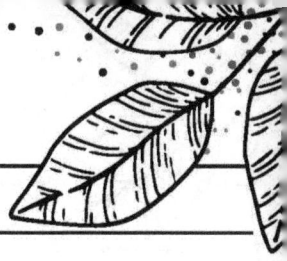

Elder 2:

How much did a gallon of gas cost when you first learned to drive?

Elder 1:

Elder 2:

Have you ever lost touch with someone who you wish you could see again?

Elder 1:

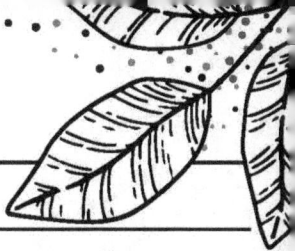

Elder 2:

What are three things about your life that bring you pure joy?

Elder 1:

Elder 2:

What were you taught, or wish you were taught, about money?

Elder 1:

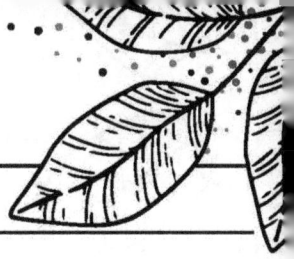

Elder 2:

What song reminds you of your childhood?

Elder 1:

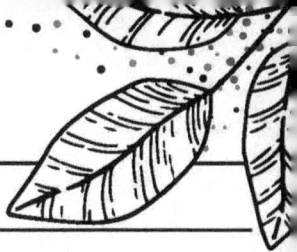

Elder 2:

What one thing has been invented during your lifetime that has made your life easier?

Elder 1:

Elder 2:

Who are some of your heroes?

Elder 1:

Elder 2:

What do you think about before falling asleep at night?

Elder 1:

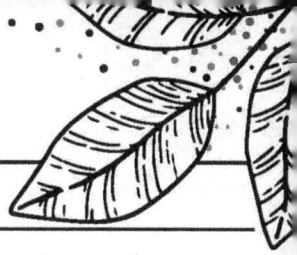

Elder 2:

What does success look like to you?

Elder 1:

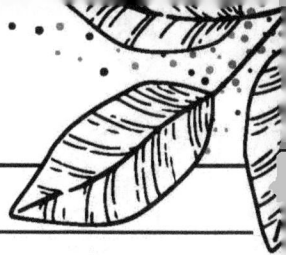

Elder 2:

What is your favorite quote or what is your favorite thing to say?

Elder 1:

Elder 2:

What do you think about when you spend time outside?

Elder 1:

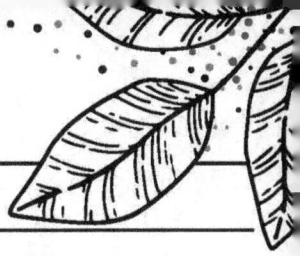

Elder 2:

What is you greatest hope for the future?

Elder 1:

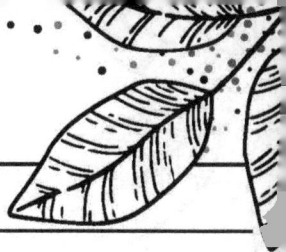

Elder 2:

If your life had a theme song, which song would be the best fit?

Elder 1:

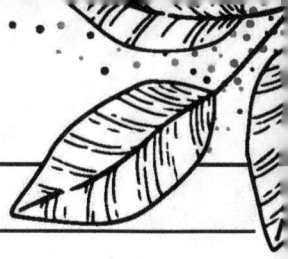

Elder 2:

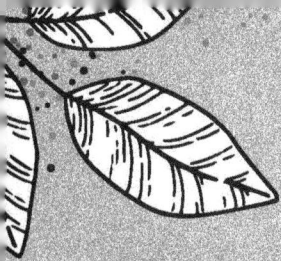

Free Write

Now that you are moving along with your conversations, you may have thought of other things you want to know.

Use the following pages to ask more questions and to learn more!

Question 1:

Elder 1:

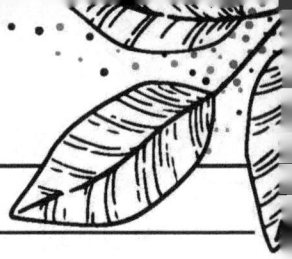

Elder 2:

Question 2:

Elder 1:

Elder 2:

Question 3:

Elder 1:

Elder 2:

Question 4:

Elder 1:

Elder 2:

Question 5:

Elder 1:

Elder 2:

Question 6:

Elder 1:

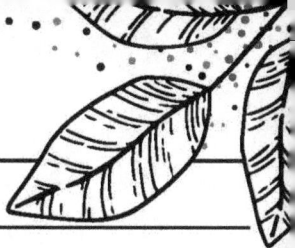

Elder 2:

Question 7:

Elder 1:

Elder 2:

Question 8:

Elder 1:

Elder 2:

Question 9:

Elder 1:

Elder 2:

Question 10:

Elder 1:

Elder 2:

www.ingramcontent.com/pod-product-compliance
Lightning Source LLC
Chambersburg PA
CBHW031548260326
41914CB00002B/329